AGILE LIFE

Understanding Agile in a non-software context

Jimmy Kidaram

Dedicated to my Parents who are the first and most influential teachers of my life ii

Let's Keep It Simple

Preface

About this book

Agility is the ability to respond to changes. It is not a concept applicable to certain industries. It is much more than that. Agile is a way of life. We should "be" Agile rather than "do" Agile. Many positive thoughts, examples, interpretations, and insights come to light when helping Agile enthusiasts on their way forward. This is an attempt to capture a few of them.

In this book, we discuss the Agile manifesto and principles. Usually when we discuss "Agile," we do it from a user–customer–provider perspective and mostly around software development. Coming out of this traditional practice, we have tried to discuss it in a layman's language. We are trying to take Agile outside the boundaries of software development. This book has some examples related to project management, but I have ensured that they are taken from life so that everyone understands.

You will not find keywords such as "Agile" or direct mentions to the Agile manifesto in the chapters except in the pages dedicated to it. But, the chapters follow a sequence, which allows the readers to easily correlate to the Agile manifesto and principles. As stated earlier, we did not restrict this discussion to the Agile manifesto because we prefer to take this tour with a free mind, without any set boundaries for our imagination.

This is an independent attempt to discuss some facts of our daily life. The opinions in this book are purely our interpretations of the world around us. Let's start our tour.

Is this book for you?

This book is for everyone who can read. Those who are familiar with Agile software development will relate the chapters to some of its key concepts. But, this is not a book on software. Previous Agile or software development knowledge of any sort is not a prerequisite to read this. Here, we discuss some incidents, experiences, and stories from daily life, that's all. Let's keep it straight and simple.

Contents

1
Steps That Never End

1. Steps That Never End

Howzaaat!!!

"Why the ***," screamed the batsman on strike at the nonstriker. They escaped a run-out narrowly. "The ball had passed the 30-yard circle with no fielders around," the nonstriker replied. "No buddy, it was my call and the best fielder was rushing there."

Let's try to create an algorithm to decide whether we should have taken a run. I guess the first criterion was that the ball has reached a decent distance. And, there were no fielders near the ball who could hit the stumps before we completed the run. Was that enough? No, not at all. What if the ball was travelling fast to a fielder with strong legs and arms? What if my partner was not in a position to run? What if the nonstriker was a slow runner or was tired after spending a long time at the crease?

We may be able to find foolproof steps for the decision. But, it may take us many generations. When we address one problem, many other new problems arise, which need to be accommodated. It is not possible to include all the conditions that may arise. However, many steps that we include have been rarely or never used.

Let's assume we have created such an algorithm and all the players have super computers fitted that can run through these steps in a fraction of a second. Even then, they may not be in sync because the perceptions and inputs that they give to the algorithm may differ.

Point of sale

One of my friends got back from a business trip and was sharing his experience. Let's not worry about the name of the city that he visited, it doesn't matter. He was speaking about his experience with a point of sale (POS) executive in a major retail chain there. He had picked out the things he wanted to buy and reached the checkout counter. The retailer follows a defined process for billing, and the executive has to follow that. It starts with greeting the customer. Then, the executive asks, "Can I bill these items?" Followed by the next question, "Would you like to buy a carry bag?" He will then bill the items and tell the customer the total amount and ask him about the payment mode. These steps will continue, and in the end, the POS executive will thank the customer and wish him a good day or night.

This worked well for him until his last visit to the shop. On the last day of visit, when he was checking out, the POS executive started the process and completed the first steps. When he was billing, my friend went to a nearby rack and picked up a pack of cookies. In the meantime, the POS executive had completed the billing and told him the bill amount. But, my friend wanted to buy the cookies as well. The executive thought for a few seconds on how to accommodate this. The software used at the counter had the option to add more items, but how would the process be followed. Finally, he decided to finish the current check out including payment and restarted the process again. He greeted once again and followed up with the questions.

This was an extreme case. But, most times people strictly follow steps, processes, and algorithms. It brings a lot of discipline and predictability to life. But, sometimes it becomes an overhead. The POS executive was doing his job and was obtaining predictable results. There was nothing wrong with what he did. He complied with the procedure and helped the customer check out. But, things could have been better.

Tailpiece

There is a limit to the amount of information that we can accommodate in documents or written steps. In our first example, a quick personal assessment of the situation and a quick communication through eye contact would have worked more effectively than any step. Having a good process at the POS is essential, because it brings in discipline. But, it should not create an overhead. A process should accommodate understanding, appreciating, and facilitating personal interactions. If we try to create foolproof steps, then an entire lifetime won't be enough to make it and the entire world won't be big enough to accommodate it. We should depend more on interactions among people and their collective strength.

Knowledge resides in people's minds. There is a limit to what we can write down on paper. We can't document everything we learn through our experiences. But, we communicate it to those who are around us and interact with us. We have many concepts supporting this thought such as work shadowing and on-the-job training. When people collaborate and work together new ideas come up and innovation happens. We have invented many tools for communication and collaboration. But, these can't replace human interactions. These tools can support, but not replace conversations.

2
Show Me the Value

2. Show Me the Value

A retrospective thought

When I started working on this book, one of the concerns was its small size. How many pages should a normal book contain? The book has approximately 200 pages and each page has approximately 300 words. But, we have only 16 small topics to discuss. Even after including the first and last chapters, it won't reach that target. What do I do in this situation? Try to expand the topics as much as I can. Make each chapter around fifteen pages long. But, the contents and the philosophy that the book is trying to preach stopped me.

What is the priority here, the number of pages or the contents of the book? What is the message that the book is trying to convey? How many pages are required to convey it? If 16 pages can convey this effectively, then let it be a 16-page book. The evaluation should be based on the value it gives, not by the number of pages.

Remember the days when we started using credit cards. Once the bank approved it, it usually was couriered to the mailing address. It arrived in a thick cover containing a lot of documents. Some were user manuals, terms and conditions, advertisements, offers, etc. Sometimes, it had several feedback forms that we would fill in after a few months of use. How many of them were useful to me, not many. Perhaps under some extreme conditions, some of them may have been useful. But, by that time it might have been already misplaced or discarded as garbage. What gives us real value is the credit card, which we have to search and find among these documents.

The invitation

"Hi, I am getting married." She was waving a large, newspaper-sized cover at me. That was her marriage invitation. A wide variety of invitation cards can be found in India. In Bangalore, there is a big street involved in this business. If you visit it, then you will seriously doubt if a majority of Bangalore's innovative quotient is invested in invitation cards rather than information technology. You get whatever you wish for. If it is not readily available, then they will make it for you within a few days or few hours. Some people look for variety and innovation, different shapes, music, surprises, etc. Some others look for size and add-ons. I accepted her invitation and appreciated the big, beautiful card. I had a quick look at it and kept it aside.

The day before the marriage we referred to the card only to confirm the date and place. This is true for most of these cards; people read it only twice, when receiving it and when going to the function. The card was beautifully designed and was full of text and images. It had very interesting quotes and a well-framed sentence, which invited me and my family to the function. But, what I was looking for is the place and route map. I couldn't find enough information in there. It was given as "ABC Mandap, XYZ halli." Bangalore is full of "Nagar's" and "Halli's." I searched the big, newspaper-sized invitation for any landmark that could lead me to the place, but there was no such information. The card had abundant information, but failed to give the useful information.

Tailpiece

How should we measure our success? It should be based on the value we add. A book with thousand pages is of no use unless it provides the intended knowledge. We can make the invitation big and beautiful, but it should not miss the intended information.

Two questions can answer this. What is the primary goal of the work that we are doing? What percentage of the final product is directly contributing to it? A bundle of manuals, contracts, and design documents will help us in executing the work, but what gives more value to the person who spends money is the working product. It doesn't mean that documents are not required. It has value and it should support the product. We should give the highest priority to the product itself.

3
The War of Clauses

3. The War of Clauses

Making it flexible

Our dream house is under construction. We had entered a contract based on square feet area. For every square foot of wall and floor, we have to pay a particular amount to the contractor. Many parameters are included in the contract, such as thickness of walls and roof and type of bricks and cement. In usual practice, river sand is used to prepare the concrete mixture. But thanks to some environmental issues, the availability of river sand reduced and it became costlier too. So, people started mixing rock powder with river sand in healthy proportions. This has become a usual practice now.

After a few days, we noticed that the contractor was using more rock powder than the appropriate measure. We brought this to his notice. But, according to him this didn't damage the construction. Yet, we disagreed. He claimed that he was not violating the contract. Therefore, we proposed that we would provide the materials, and we would change the contract to state that he provides only labor. But, he refused and our relationship got damaged. In the end, we fired him and entered a new contract with a different company.

It was a well-written and time-tested contract. Yet, it was not flexible enough to adapt to the situation. The rigid nature of the contract made it nearly impossible to address unexpected situations. Also, it had taken away the transparency and given way to a tense situation.

The online store

My family doesn't prefer buying groceries and vegetables online. We prefer to walk to the nearest shop and pick our required commodities. But the online shops were gaining momentum, and we didn't want to be left behind. We decided to give it a try. Attracted by their same day delivery option, we selected a new vendor from the local market. I selected all the items and placed the order. There was an option to pay on delivery, but the payment was made using credit card.

We were happy to see the delivery boy at our doorstep within a couple of hours. It was pretty fast. We received the items and an invoice. I did not check the invoice because we had already paid online. But when unpacking, I was surprised to find two items missing. Our first reaction was to check the invoice. The delivered items matched the invoice. But, two items were missing from my original order. I thought this possibly was the first part of the delivery and another person would deliver the remaining items. Anyway, I decided to call the vendor and confirm.

"Sir, I apologize for the inconvenience. We have modified your order as a few items were out of stock" was the reply from the call center executive. "We had sent you an email regarding the same within a few minutes after you placed the order."

"What the ####, do you expect me to check my emails all the time? First, if it is out of stock, you shouldn't allow anyone to select it. And, if you are changing my order, you should call me up and ascertain to inform me before delivery."

"Sorry Sir, according to the process you have agreed to when placing the order let us modify the order. You agreed to this process. We regret the inconvenience; we will return your amount in 2 days."

Again, the procedure comes in way of a better customer experience. The two items were not fast-moving commodities, and they won't be available in many shops. But, I would have continued shopping with them if they had dealt with the situation better.

Tailpiece

What went wrong with our contractor? The first contract was not flexible enough to accommodate unexpected scenarios. The contract took precedence over our needs. In the same way, the situation would have been better if the online vendor had called me and informed me about the same. I would have chosen some alternatives.

It is not the existence of the contract, but the nature of the contract that created issues. Contracts are required; it gives us the framework and the authority to do our work. It should be written to bring in more collaboration, and it should pursue a situation when a customer becomes part of the process. Frequent customer feedback is essential to build the right system.

4
The Flexibles

4. The Flexibles

Gods own country

All these times, we have been discussing not so good scenarios. Feeling a little bored about that. Let's switch to something positive. I belong to a state called Kerala. It is in the southern part of India, near the Arabian Sea. Its natural beauty and rich cultural heritage makes it an international tourist destination and is often referred to as "God's Own Country." Kerala has the highest literacy rate among Indian states and has achieved good results in public health and education.

At the same time, Kerala is a highly political state with a strong presence of communist parties. Political movements and strikes are common. One of the common methods of strike is called "Harthal." It means a total shut-down with closed shops and empty roads. I remember because it was a dark day for us. We were not able to go out as the roads were blocked and the shops were shut. Not many TV Channels were available to keep us entertained those days.

Now, the people of Kerala have learnt how to turn a "Harthal" into a celebration. Many people take advantage of the day. They get an opportunity to spend quality time with their families. Now, the moment a "Harthal" is announced, they plan their day, stock all the required items such as food, drinks, music, or movies, and are prepared for that day. I am not welcoming the concept of Harthal; it brings a lot of loss and inconvenience to the people and the state. This is merely an observation on the change in public behavior and how they have learnt to adapt to this situation.

The dynamic vendor

How often do we change the way we live? The answer may be when the situation demands or there is a need. We find many roadside vendors in Bangalore who serve many items such as tea, coffee, juices, and snacks. Trends in eating habits change with changing climate and season. But, for these small vendors it changes within a day itself. Tea sells quickly early in the morning and in the evening. Under the hot sun, it is fresh fruit juice. Late in the evening, people prefer snacks.

There was a vendor in front of our college who diversified his products with his innovation. He served different items at different times of the day. The day started with tea then juice and ended with evening snacks. He carried a thermocol box, which contained the cookies that he sold in the morning with tea. Later in the day, another vendor supplied him with ice cubes, which he stored in the same box. By evening, the box would be empty. He would keep the box open so that it became dry, warm, and ready to store cookies, the next morning.

This is a common man's humble reaction to changing environments. Certainly a man with such flexibility would be able to respond to an unexpected change as well, like if it is a rainy day. He kept things simple and that made him flexible enough.

Tailpiece

In a plan driven system, we try to visualize the end to end of the work that we take up, and we come up with a detailed plan. But in life, how many such plans remain unchanged? Perhaps, there are a few if they are really lucky. Change is the only constant and to survive we must respond to it effectively. It is the very essence of our existence.

How do we respond to change? It is by changing ourselves. We change the way we do things. Also, we change the things we do. For example, we may change the way we cook if certain ingredients are not available. Also, we may cook new dishes based on the available ingredients.

Additional Pages

Readers who are not interested in software development can skip this section and go to Chapter 5. Don't worry about this; you can pick up from Chapter 5.

Now please read the four Agile manifesto items listed in the next page. Check if we can map them to the concepts that we have discussed in the first four chapters.

Manifesto for Agile Software Development

We are uncovering better ways of developing
software by doing it and helping others do it.
Through this work we have come to value:

Individuals and interactions over processes and tools

Working software over comprehensive documentation

Customer collaboration over contract negotiation

Responding to change over following a plan

That is, while there is value in the items on
the right, we value the items on the left more.

Kent Beck	James Grenning	Robert C. Martin
Mike Beedle	Jim Highsmith	Steve Mellor
Arie van Bennekum	Andrew Hunt	Ken Schwaber
Alistair Cockburn	Ron Jeffries	Jeff Sutherland
Ward Cunningham	Jon Kern	Dave Thomas
Martin Fowler	Brian Marick	

Content in this page is referred from http://agilemanifesto.org

5
Serve Hot

5. Serve Hot

The starters

 Let's start the second part of our discussion with some delicious dishes. During the last few decades, the restaurants in Bangalore have witnessed a lot of fundamental changes. One of the important changes was that they have come a long way from being just food vendors. They not only cater to our taste buds, but also make a sincere attempt to give us a quality time. It includes many aspects from the parking to the billing, from order to the delivery, and from ambiance to hospitality.

One of the most restless periods in a restaurant is from the order to the first dish. This is not only because I am a foodie, but also it gives us a feel about the quality of the food. In our city, many restaurants still have the traditional mindset of a food vendor. They prefer to take the entire order at once and try to deliver it together. But most of the restaurants have changed this habit and have tried to reduce the initial waiting time as much as possible. The overall time taken from order to the service of our final dish on our table may remain almost the same, but they try to deliver at least a few dishes within a few minutes.

What difference does it make? They make sure something is on our table all the time. It may add to their business, and there is a good chance for us to repeat the orders. They keep us engaged by reducing the waiting time.

The emerging store

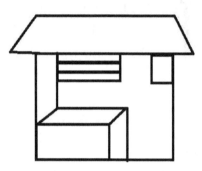 One of my relatives was about to start a business in our small township. He was planning to start a small store with only fast-moving commodities such as common groceries, stationery items for daily use, bread, and packed juices. A bank financed him, and he rented out a space as well. The space was a precondition to receive financing from the bank.

He had to start the interior work for the shop, wardrobes, racks, counters, etc., which was estimated to take a month's time. But he had already started paying the rent and the interest. He started exploring different vendors who could complete the interior work faster. The additional cost involved in buying ready-made furniture was high and did not give a reasonable reduction in the estimated time.

I asked him why he didn't start the shop now and do the interiors simultaneously. You can start shop with a few items that doesn't need all the interior work. He had the money, and he could buy a refrigerator within hours and start selling packed juices. Similarly, there were many items that he could start selling immediately. He could make it more convenient by making the furniture at home and assemble it in the shop. This would reduce the time required inside the shop for the interior work. As the work progressed, he could add more items, giving him some income right from the beginning and reducing his burden of managing cash flow.

Tailpiece

How do we analyze both these situations? What is common in both? It is an early realization of value. In the restaurant, we got going at the earliest. What is the benefit? We can list down many. We got our order sooner rather than later. We were eating even before our entire order was prepared. It gives us a time advantage. It gives us an opportunity to give an early feedback. For example, if we didn't like a certain topping or the oil we have a chance to change it in coming dishes.

In the shop story, the business value is more visible. He started making revenue early, which supported him in repaying the loan. He didn't have to wait for the interior to be completed to start his business. He received an early feedback from the customer behavior, based on which he could change the design of the shop itself. Both these examples preach two points, start creating the value at the earliest and create opportunities for early feedback.

6
In This Dynamic World

6. In This Dynamic World

The smart builder

 How flexible is your industry toward the changes in customer requirements? It depends on the type of industry and the way customers behave. In the real estate business, we can't change a 10-storied building to a 20-storied one, late in the construction phase. We might have already built the foundation for a ten level building. But, we may be able to convert a movie hall to a general auditorium easily.

This happened recently in a nearby town. Toward the end of constructing the structure, the promoters estimated the ROIs and decided go for a "Kalyana Mandapa," an auditorium for marriage receptions, rather than a movie hall. It was not their flexible planning that enabled them to make his decision. Actually, it was their constraints that made them flexible. They were facing some cash flow problems; therefore, they were funding the construction just in time, in phases. They had not finalized the deal for costly equipment like a projector in advance. So, the financial loss was less except for a few unwanted counters in the premises.

Their approach was a flexible one, even though it was built in unintentionally. It gives us a good reason to believe that we can be flexible toward the end if we plan smart. This is applicable even in those industries, which are otherwise considered very rigid to the changes. We always say that we should keep an eye on the changing conditions and check its impact. But, we often forget that these evaluations result in changes, which we have to accommodate in our work. So, we have to plan our work smartly to embrace these changes.

The postal service

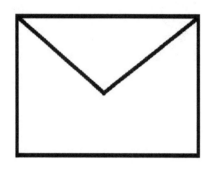 I often wondered why the providers in the private sector scored better than those in the public sector, even when their rates were much higher. First answer that anyone gives would be quality. I prefer to be more specific by saying, the way they deliver quality. Let's take an example.

"ABC Post," a traditional postal system, has existed since a long time. It was the only provider until the government opened up this business to private investors. It is supported by huge infrastructure and enjoys a wide reach. It is well-staffed with offices in every corner of the country. It offers cheap rates, and we can trust the delivery as well. Yet, it is losing to its competitors. Many people prefer new players, unless there is a huge difference in pricing.

I was expecting a parcel via ABC Post. I tracked it online to see it reached an office nearby from where it was supposed to get delivered to my residence. I waited for a few more days and I did not receive the item. With a lot of difficulty, I managed to call their office. They told me that they came to my house and I was not there. Now, if I want it, then I have to collect it from their office. Also, before going there I should call the concerned person to ensure that he is available.

What followed is not relevant here. Let's try to compare. What could have been a better scenario? On seeing my house locked, they could have called me. I work in an office near my house and they could have delivered it there. There is nothing wrong in what they did. They followed the rules, but failed to show a little flexibility that could have helped me a lot, without any extra cost.

Tailpiece

How flexible should we be in accommodating changes? The answer will depend on the work that we do. But, it is clear that there will be many changes. We are living in an environment where change is the only constant. So, change is an expected situation not an exceptional scenario.

There are many practices that enable us to respond effectively to the changes. We can plan for a short duration, so that we can accommodate the changes before planning for the next duration. We can evaluate our work against the parameters so that we can find the deviations early. We can regularly reassess the environment where we work, so that any interesting developments can be identified at the earliest. All these practices group around a simple theory. When developing anything, a change in the early stage is easier than in the later stage. We produce early results and continuously to allow early inspection and reduce the cost of making the change.

Another aspect that enhances our flexibility is an excellent and extensible design. An excellent design doesn't mean a complex one. A simple design is enough to address our requirements, which can be enhanced further.

Also, we should design our processes in a way that addresses unexpected scenarios. It should be flexible enough to respond to changes.

7
Keep Them Awake

7. Keep Them Awake

Reporting from the war zone

It was during a business trip to one of our client locations. My task was to understand their challenges if any and propose solutions. It was a 2-week trip. The usual practice was to hold discussions, make observations, and note down the points during these weeks; come back; consolidate; and present a report after internal reviews. I had to present within a couple of days after my visit, before the client changed his mind. So, the days after the trips always turned out to be demanding ones. A Lot of work, reviews, and presentations flying around, unexpected changes proposed by my reviewer, etc.

I decided to do things differently this time. So, I started working on the presentation from the first day of the visit. At the end of day, a consolidated list of observations and suggestions was sent to the reviewer. I was expecting an appreciative reply from him for my proactive step. But there was no reply to my mail. On the second day, the deck was updated again and sent to him. This time I called him. He was under the perception that this was going to be extra effort because we would have to do it again at the end of the visit. I tried to convince him of the benefits of this incremental approach.

He was not very convinced, but thanks to the good work relationship we shared, he agreed to spend some time on it every day. With each day he grew more and more involved in this practice. At the end of my visit, our presentation was almost 70% ready, and we prepared the remaining presentation on the very next day. Without any tension or loss of sleep, we were able to put on a better presentation this time. And more interestingly, next trip onwards the reviewer started requesting for this approach.

What I did was simply attempt an early and continuous delivery of value. It helped me get early feedback. We realized the problems early. It avoided tense days and last-minute rush.

Time sheets

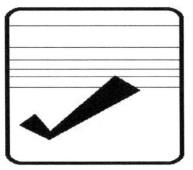

We don't have to look up and wide to find good examples of better practice. We can find so many in our daily life. There are many small things that we can do in a great way.

How many times has your salary gotten delayed because you have not filled your time sheet on time? May not be very frequent, must be a very rare scenario. But, how many times have you ended up filling time sheets for the entire month on the last day? I am sure to see many hands raised on this question. I faced it many times. It may look very simple, but it can have unexpected impact as well. What will happen if you are totally tied up on the last day and you have to catch a flight in the evening? What if your computer crashes? Workarounds and solutions exist, and we can improve the scene.

No prizes for guessing the solution. Everyone knows we should fill our time sheets frequently and incrementally. If not every day, then do it every week at least. Many employers try to impose it as a better practice. But, how many of us religiously follow it? This is a small step that adds a small but significant value to our life.

Tailpiece

First example shows how an incremental approach has given me peace of mind toward the end of the period. Second example is as simple as avoiding the overload at the end of the month. Both these examples emphasize the power of early and constant feedback. What do we understand from this? We can avoid creating something without knowing if it is good or bad. If we fail, then we fail early and we have enough time to rectify our mistakes. It keeps all those who are in the system awake and involved. It in turn creates a shared ownership. It reduces risk as the feedback is early and frequent.

8
Over the Boundaries

8. Over the Boundaries

Making your plate

Food and restaurants always make interesting examples when we discuss topics related to business or customer dynamics. Let's not break that tradition. So, grab your lunch.

Let's try comparing two food chains and their delivery process. Let's consider a pizza vendor and the other deals with subs. When we walk in to pizza store, we are welcomed by a colorful menu displayed in the background. There are many varieties and sizes that we can choose from. We can make our choice and order it at the counter. We are asked to choose the extra toppings and add-ons like fries and soft drinks. Once we have made up our minds and place the order, our job is done. We wait for 10–15 minutes and before we start eating the delicious pizza. This is a good example of engaging the customer by customizing a product based on their requirements.

Now, let's talk about the Subs store. The environment is almost the same. We find attractive displays and friendly staff. But, here there is one difference. We are not making all choices in advance and placing the order. Instead, we are invited to be part of the process. First, we are asked to choose the type of the bread and its size. Then, we are told to choose the vegetables and it will be placed on the bread right in front of our eyes. We are then shown different types of meats to create the middle layer. It goes on like this. The product is made right in front of us based on our preferences. We are able to see it emerge and make our choices on the fly.

Both these businesses are good examples of customer engagement. Which one has an edge? It depends on the type of product and nature of the customer.

The samosa chain

Sounds weird? Yes, I mean it. We often discuss famous supply chains, distribution networks, and market studies. But, there are more effective systems operating around us. Samosa is a delicious vegetarian snack item; it is cheap and easily available in Bangalore and most Indian cities. It has a shelf-life of only 2 days. It is available at almost all small to medium vendors in our city.

It got into my head that I should understand how they work. Every day I saw a man in our area distributing samosas to the shops nearby. I got in touch with him and found out that every morning he buys his stock from a wholesale vendor near the market. The samosas are made during the night and reach this vendor early in the morning. He takes it from there and completes the distribution before the city is in full swing.

These people don't use any computers or smart phones. They have obtained minimum levels of literacy and know only the local language. But, still they maintain proper inventory levels and reduce wastage. The entire show is run by good coordination and effective handshakes. The only data collected is the answer to a magical question that he asks the retailer, "Eshtu balance?" or how many remain? This is the only data they use to decide how many pieces he needs for the day and how much he should order for tomorrow. This information moves up in the chain and reaches as an estimated demand to the kitchen. They recalculate the demand every day. There is communication between all four stake holders, the retailer, supplier, wholesale vendor, and those who run the kitchen. If we explore more, we can add more into this chain like those who provide ingredients to the kitchen. All of them coordinate effectively every day.

It is not the technology or the individual brilliance that matters. It is how effectively we put things together that matters at the end of the day.

Tailpiece

Both these examples discuss collaboration among different layers in the system. First example is a good example of user involvement that creates earlier feedback. It reduces wastage. As the product is created in front of our eyes, we can easily express what we require. It reduces any deviation of the end product from what is expected. In the second story, we can see an effective coordination from the retailer to the kitchen. A handshake on a daily basis enables them to run their business more effectively. This simple philosophy is applicable everywhere from samosa to satellite when more than one person is part of the system.

9
Trust Them First

9. Trust Them First

The Yellow Page

An error page displayed by a web browser where the text is highlighted in yellow was referred to as a "Yellow Page." It indicated that something had gone wrong when loading the page. I am not sure if web browsers work in the same lines now, but it was something of concern in the earlier days.

This happened a few years back. It was lunchtime, and we were about to head out for lunch when I got a message from my boss. "Jimmy, we are getting a yellow page when trying to load the new changes. I have managed to take them for lunch now. But, please have a look." A demonstration was being undertaken for a prospective client. We had made a few changes to the product in the demonstration according to the client needs. My boss was giving the presentation, and he was shocked to find that the new pages were not working. But somehow, he managed to call for a break and take the clients out for lunch. This was the background of the call.

We managed to fix it before they came back from lunch. It was a silly mistake I made, and I was prepared for some nice words from my lead. I was thinking that my day was ruined. In the evening, he walked to my desk. "Jimmy, we did a good job. The presentation was a great success." And he went on to talk about future plans. When we were about to leave he said, "Thanks for that quick fix at the lunchtime. We will try doing it a bit early henceforth."

He did not try to place blame. Instead, he trusted me to get it fixed even when it was a clear mistake on my part. The discussion would have been completely different if he did not have the right mindset. What was the result? The support that he gave me on my bad day was a positive signal for the entire team. In return, he got more commitment and loyalty from our side.

Be a good buddy

 We were invited for lunch by one of our relatives. They had recently relocated from a city to the nearby village. He sold out his house in the town and bought 3 acres of agricultural land in the village, with a small wooden house along with it where he lived. It was beautiful place with a lot of greenery around, like anywhere in Kerala.

We reached his house at around 11 AM. There were two men plowing his land. In Kerala, we have different types of agriculture labor available. Most popular is the daily contract with fixed wages. Work timings are usually from 8 AM to 5 PM, with a lunch break and two tea breaks. Food is not included in the contract and the worker has to make his own arrangements. But on that day, the house owner invited them to join us for lunch. We welcomed this and appreciated him for the high values that he follows.

Before we left his house, I felt it is worth bringing the topic up again. I wanted to hear from him. He had many reasons for such a kind gesture. "Anyway I was arranging food for you. So, it wasn't much added effort for me to count them in as well. But in return, I am getting many things. They are not going out for lunch so they will resume work sooner. That is an immediate effect. Most important thing is that I am creating a strong bond with them. It may prompt them to go that extra mile for me. Tomorrow they will be happy to work for me rather than my neighbor"

Tailpiece

We don't have to go to business schools to learn management. The simple, down to earth people with real experience of life are great professors in the University of Life. A smile or a pat on the back can be very effective. Always be available for the team and provide them with what they require. And, off course trust them. The trust given by my lead motivated us to do a better work. Many times teams need support. Be proactive to understand their needs and address it. It doesn't mean that there should not be any inspection. First, empower the team to inspect themselves. Inspect the team to empower them but not to punish them.

There are two dimensions here: capability and trust. A team should get whatever is required to carry out the work in hand. It can be their capabilities, the infrastructure, or a good environment to work in. And, we should trust them to get the work done.

10
It Sounds Better

10.   It Sounds Better

Leave Application

 "At last, I got it done," my friend told me with a sigh of relief. "It has been a week. He was delaying it with many unnecessary questions." He was talking about his leave application that was approved. It sounded interesting to me as I have never faced a delay for such a decision. I decided to check what happened. During lunchtime the same topic came up. The story went like this.

He was planning a 2-week vacation. The leave application was submitted well in advance and he had made alternative arrangements for work as well. His manager replied by mail asking him if it is possible for him to shorten the leave by 1 week. Stating valid reasons, he politely expressed his inability to do so. After a day, he got an email requesting him to postpone it by a month. But he had already made all the arrangements and it was difficult for him to change his plans. He informed the same to the manager again via mail. Then, the next topic was his back up plans. In short, the discussion took a week to complete.

This is a common practice among most people sitting on their computers all the time. For us it is easier to click on a reply button than pick up a receiver to make a call. We don't even think about walking to the nearest building to talk to someone in person. The above process could have been completed within minutes if a better mode of communication was used.

On your face

It was on a return journey from Kochi to Bangalore. The airlines announced a delay in the flight timings and I was waiting in the airport. There was a gentleman siting a few chairs ahead. His face looked very familiar and I recognized him as someone I met during one of the seminars in Bangalore. He was a very friendly and receptive personality. I thought of renewing our contact. So, we got into a chat over tea.

He told that he was there to conduct training for one of his teams working out of Kochi.

"Oh ... So, you were in Kochi for some time?"

"No," he replied, "I came today. It was a half day event."

I was a little surprised. Why did he have to travel for this? It is within the organization and we have new technologies at our disposal. We could do an audio bridge or a WebEx instead. He just smiled at me as a reply.

It was a long wait and I grabbed a magazine from the stand and got absorbed in that. "Jimmy." He woke me up from my thoughts. "Are you using this model by any chance?" I saw him holding his mobile phone in one hand and a SIM card on the other. He was looking at the device. "No," I replied, "But, I know how to change the SIM. We need a small needle like stuff to remove the old SIM out."

"It's okay, Jimmy." I saw the same smile on his face again. "I just needed to tell you something. I asked you a very simple question, but you answered to much more than what I have asked you. What is the reason?"

That was his answer to my earlier question. The long answer I gave was not a reply to the question that I had heard; it was for the question that I had seen. A commonly used and famous philosophy states that a good part of the communications happens non-verbally. He found training to be more effective when he can deliver it in person. It gave him an opportunity to interact with the team, and he received the feedback immediately. He could improvise his delivery on stage, which undoubtedly is more effective.

Tailpiece

The main constructs in any communication are the sender, the recipient, and the medium. The sender initiates communication and sends it across to the recipient through the medium. The recipient receives it and sends the acknowledgement. The sender gets the acknowledgement to confirm that the communication is success. All these steps happen simultaneously in a face-to-face conversation. So, it is considered the most effective way of communication.

Face-to-face conversations reduce all the disturbances that can happen because of technology. This reduces feedback time. A sender can adjust his messages spontaneously based on the response that he receives. There are many tools in the market ranging from a simple desk phone to technically advanced video presence rooms. All these can enhance the way we communicate and at times simulate face-to-face conversations. But they have their limitations, the main one being the noise in the medium. So, irrespective of the tools the power of face-to-face conversations remains unquestioned.

11
Measure the Fence Not the Trench

11. Measure the Fence Not the Trench

Count the value

"What are you going to do with these ten pages? Don't you feel it is too short for a presentation?" I could feel that my boss was really upset. I was supposed to present our plan for a very short engagement to our client.

"But James, this is all that we have to present. I have included all that we have to convey in this meeting"

He was not convinced. "Why can't you add a few slides on their organization? It will give them a good feeling that we know about them." I was shocked to hear this answer. He was asking me to tell the client about themselves. That was nowhere in scope of the presentation. Many of us might have already faced such a scenario owing to the people around us or something ingrained within us. People tend to rate based on the quantity not the quality.

When I work as a coach, I measure it based on the effectiveness of my team and how they have improved. But, when I train for a certification the measurement becomes more quantitative as how many of them have reached the knowledge levels and successfully completed the certification.

We should concentrate on the value created by an activity that we are doing. We put in a lot of effort and time. But, what do we achieve? What value do we add to the system? That is what matters at the end of the day.

The beauty cream ad

 Should I strengthen my bones or reduce my tummy? Should I concentrate on growing my hair or reducing stress? Does the boy need more height or more memory? There are too many choices and difficult decisions to make. This is an era of advertisements. Many of our decisions are controlled by advertising giants.

It is hard to believe what they say, but I saw an interesting advertisement that went on air recently. It was for a fairness cream. They claimed that your complexion improves by four units within 2 weeks. The units are defined by them. But, what made it interesting for me is that they provided a measuring scale with the cream. We have to mark our current score in the scale. And, every day we could measure and record our progress.

Yes, there will be a "conditions apply" tag line and conditions in such small letters that nobody can read. I am not sure how effective the cream is; maybe I can let you know in a few days. But, I liked the concept of including a scale with the product. They invited the customer to measure their product based on the value it provides.

I have many good friends who are always concerned about my health and have advised me to start working out every day. "Jimmy, check this out. It is very easy you can do it in 15 minutes." "No man, you should try this. You can do this at home, and it takes only 10 minutes." "This is the best. You can do it sitting on your chair." Many options came from many corners. All of them are talking about short time duration and the ease of performing. But, what is the real intention of working out, and how will it help me? Are they missing the main idea?

How do we measure a product or a service? No questions, it should be based on how well the product provides us with the intended benefits. I will choose an airline that takes off on time rather than the one that plays my favorite movies.

Tailpiece

As we have discussed in one of the earlier chapters, it is the value that matters. Our work should be evaluated based on the value we have created. It is not the number pages in the presentation, it is the relevance and the use of information that it provides. It is not the cost, color, or fragrance of the beauty cream that interests the clients, but it is the improvement that it brings to your skin that matters.

12
The Golden Goose

12.   The Golden Goose

The marathon runner

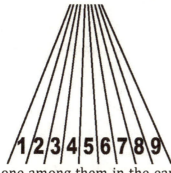

How long can a cheetah maintain its speed? Don't think it is for a long time. We can find many cheetahs in our daily life. They start with high speed and high volume, but are worn out before they reach the destination. I was one among them in the early stages of my career. I rarely went back home; I used to be at office most of the times. Many times, I spent days together in my office. The idea was to finish off the work and relax. But, work never ended and I stayed in the office.

I was not able to continue the same for long. My work and personal life was getting affected. And, people started expecting those high volumes from me, which I was producing during the first few days of my cheetah run. I was not able to maintain the same speed for a long period. My performance stopped meeting their expectations, and I was not able to continue there for a long time.

What I was missing there was the strategy of a marathon runner. He never burns out his energy in the first few laps itself. He keeps a consistent momentum that he can sustain for a long time. I could have planned my work with realistic estimates based on my daily capacities so that I could sustain it indefinitely.

The spike times

What will happen if we use one horse and a cow for the same chariot? It's the same old classic question. Here, we are talking about parallel forces that should be operating in tandem. Can we relate it to sequential processing? If we take a relay run it will not have much impact. But, what will be the impact on an order - production - delivery chain?

All these functions should work in good sync. Orders should not overload production beyond its capacity. We should limit the production based on the delivery system. What is wrong if we have a huge inventory of ready to ship products in our warehouse? Doesn't it give enough supply to our delivery system? We don't have to worry about the availability. We often forget that it comes with a cost. A huge inventory is always money stuck in our production line. We don't realize the value until it is delivered. In the same way, if we put more pressure on the production it won't be able to sustain the momentum for long.

We can find many examples in our daily life. Towards the end of the financial year we can find a huge rush in most of the offices. There are many bills pending for clearance, many products pending approval, etc. We always tend to keep the last date as our rule. It is a common compliant from the quality department of any industry that they get too much work towards the end and have to stretch the day. But, all other times they were relatively idle. What will be the impact? Without any doubt we can say that the quality will get affected.

What is missing in all these examples? We are missing a holistic big picture. We sit in our cubicle and forget the fact that we are part of a bigger system that has to deliver. We should try to optimize the entire system for which we should work in sync with other parts.

Tailpiece

This reminds us about the famous tale of the Golden Goose. We must not kill the Golden Goose thinking that we can run away with all the golden eggs at once. We should try to get in a small amount every day consistently. This is applicable in our work as well. Don't try to overload the system, it will wear out. Adjust the load in such a way that it is sustainable for a long period.

A sustainable pace will bring in quality. It brings quality to the lives of those who are working in the system. It brings quality into the system and the products coming out of it. Quality will suffer if overloaded workers try to focus more on completion.

13
Be Solid to be Flexible

13. Be Solid to be Flexible

Play it on

I am a fan of pre-owned cars. It gives a lot of flexibility. It gives me an opportunity to change my car when I wish. The rate of depreciation is less and I break even early. In my short life, so far I have never bought a new car. I was living happily with my oldies until the recent past.

Road accidents were increasing in the city and authorities had decided to tighten the screws. They started coming down heavily on traffic violations including use of cell phones when driving. Adding to the situation, the central government proposed a revision of charges. Fines went up from a few hundreds to ten thousand. I usually answer calls when driving using my head sets. To be on the safer side I decided to switch to a Bluetooth-based system.

The music system in my car did not support Bluetooth, so I sought expert opinion. According to the advice given by one of my friends, only the front panel of the existing system needed to be changed to enable the Bluetooth device. Many panels were available from local brands for different types of cars. I took my car to a shop recommended by my friend. But, things didn't go well for me. The mechanic told me that the existing system in the car didn't support panel replacement. We had to change the entire assembly as the panel is not detachable in this version. The existing system already had an AUX input slot. That meant it has a cable to receive audio input and give it to the main unit. If the design involved a detachable head panel, then we could have easily modified it to accommodate other types of inputs as well.

The buff

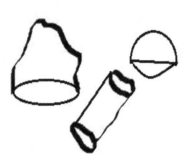

What does technical excellence mean to you? When we hear the word "technical excellence" many pictures flash in our minds like rockets, satellites, planes, space ships, and designs with many wires. But, a simple small design also can achieve this designation.

I always have a tough time shopping for head gear. Be it a helmet, band, skull-cap, or a simple hat. Searching in branded and local shops would end with empty shopping bags, and it took a lot of time before I found something. Most times I don't get to choose.

Recently, I bought a new product. It may have been in the markets for some time, but I saw it for the first time. Don't worry it was not something to trim my skull; it was a simple tube with stretchable cloth. It can be stretched only width wise and the length remained fixed. We call this product Buff. It has many other names as well. The beauty of the product was that we can wear it many ways. We could make it into many types of hats or skullcaps. Some internet videos claim to explain around 50 ways of using it. Anyway what I needed was a cap, so I learnt a few ways of using it as a cap.

It is a simple product that solves a small problem. But, I believe the idea behind it is worth a "thumbs up."

Tailpiece

A simple two piece design could have avoided changing the entire set in my car. But, there may be many other trade-offs that acted as deciding forces against that. The simple design makes a buff flexible to be used in many ways. But, there was an excellent feature embedded in its simplicity. It was stretchable only width wise not length wise, which made it flexible.

But, how much effort should we put in a design to make it excellent? There is a trade-off. We don't know what will happen in the future, the detailed designs that we make may become obsolete tomorrow. So, we have to concentrate in balancing these forces. We should work on the design enough, but it should have quality. There is a famous saying that there are days when we do great things, but every day we can do small things in a great way. So, make it simple and make it excellent.

14
Keep It Simple

14.   Keep It Simple

The alphabet game

Let's try to make our discussion a little more interesting with a game. It is a group activity introduced to a group of 10 IT professionals. It went like this...

Participants were asked to create alphabet cards they can use to spell out names. Instead of shouting the letters, they had to show the card. They were not required to create duplicates, as they could use the same alphabet card multiple times. They arranged themselves and divided the letters among themselves and started working on the task. They did a good job and completed the activity on time. All 26 letters were ready and arranged in line. And, we were ready to go.

We wrote all the 26 letters on the whiteboard. Participants started spelling their first names by showing the cards one by one. As a group, we started counting based on the letters in our names. We wanted to find out the number of times that each letter was being used. For example, if the given name was "Jimmy," then one point each for J, I, and Y, and two for M were counted. Let's say the next person gives the name "Tommy." We will add one for T and O and increased the count for Y to two and M to four. This exercise was repeated for all the participants.

Then, we arranged the letters in the descending order of the count. Eleven letters were unused, four letters were used only once, and two letters were used twice.

This is a common scenario associated with almost every system that we come across. It may be a software application or a mobile phone. It can be the items that we buy or the house that we build. Many of the features will remain unused or rarely used.

Shopping for Goa

Since I started writing this book, all that happens around me appears to be related to these topics in some way or the other. Maybe that's how a human mind works.

Last week, I got a call from one of my friends asking if I am interested in a vacation in Goa. I didn't have any reason to refuse. The discussion started among seven close families and we agreed to schedule it somewhere toward the end of next month. We started working on the itinerary.

All this happened a few days before we were shopping on our weekend. My wife came up with a great idea. We were getting a good discount now. Why didn't we shop for our Goa trip too? The idea appeared to be interesting to me as well. But luckily a second thought struck my mind. We, friends, were very volatile with our plans, and we had not finalized the travel. So, there was a good chance of cancelling the plan.

"Don't you think we are buying it a bit early?" She was not prepared for this question, clearly written on her face. We will get a few hundreds rupees of discount now. But, if the trip got cancelled or if our destination changed, then all that we buy would become useless. She was not really convinced, but I was successful in confusing her. So, we decided to postpone the shopping for Goa.

It is a common question; when should I do an activity? The old school tells us "the sooner the better" or "ASAP." It is difficult to accept this ASAP philosophy as universally acceptable? We should be smart in timing our activities. Sometimes an intentional delay gives better results.

Tailpiece

There is a thin line between laziness and intelligent delays. It was not laziness that delayed our shopping. It was a strong belief that there were chances that an idea can change and it was too early to start working on it. The alphabet game shows the importance of prioritizing the work that we do. In both cases, we are not avoiding anything. We are postponing certain activities, because there are activities of higher priority that we have to do now. We have to concentrate on creating frequently used letters than the unused ones. We should try to finalize the itinerary before shopping.

If we state the same in another way, then we should avoid creating unused letters before all the useful ones are created. We should avoid shopping for Goa before the trip is confirmed. In other words, we can avoid wastage by postponing the uncertain activities until the last moment.

15
Tap the Synergy

15. Tap the Synergy

My innovative cousins

With a few drops of tears and a mind full of prayers let me recollect an incident that happened during my grandfather's funeral. Our parish church and the cemetery were near a small township and our house was a few kilometers away from it. The funeral took place on a Sunday afternoon. We have a custom of serving tea after the funeral service for those who attended it.

My father requested a few of my uncles to make arrangements for the tea. They reached the town for the same. But, most shops remained closed on a Sunday. They went to a caterer, but he was extremely busy that afternoon. There was a restaurant open, but they didn't have anything other than packed food because of slow business on a Sunday afternoon. They returned home empty-handed.

But, my father didn't want to break the custom. So, my cousins decided to give it a try. They rushed to the township and spoke to the restaurant owner and convinced him to make the tea if they brought the required items. They went to the few nearby shops that were open and arranged for milk powder and tea leaves. When the tea was being prepared, they approached the caterer and rented out a big flask to store the tea and bought disposable glasses. All this was done in an hour, and tea reached the church premises well in time. They played the role of the caterer and served the tea themselves.

This is not one of the greatest tasks in this world. But, this small task was completed with proper organization within the constraints.

Back to school

Whenever I go to work, the laptop is just one of the items in my backpack. My backpack is filled with tennis balls, balloons, post-its, color pens, playing cards, etc. I always enjoy interacting with people through games and team activities. Here is one of them.

We assembled around 30 people in a hall with enough space to move around. Each person was provided a white paper and a marker. They had to write numbers from one to hundred in the given paper. We would measure the time taken for this activity. There would be experts, but we were concerned about the time taken by the team to complete the activity, which would depend on the slowest member in the group. The team completed this activity pretty fast.

In round two, a white paper was hung behind each participant using a thread of around 50 centimeters. They could hardly pull the paper to their sides. They were given the same task. I saw a lot of creative ideas around. Someone went around in circles. Some others were kneeling down in front of the table, but were taking a lot of time. Then, we stopped this activity and gave them 5 minutes to think as a team about how they could approach this issue.

They already had some ideas in their minds when completing the previous round, so before the 5 minutes were over they came back to me saying that they were ready. I asked them to go ahead. Then, they formed a big circle and each member started writing numbers on the paper of the person standing in front. They hit the bull's-eye.

There is nothing to explain; it is a simple straightforward example of good team work. As a team they innovated and won the day.

Tailpiece

Second example shows how the team resolved an issue that they were struggling with, individually. They worked as a team. This self-organizing nature and collective thinking brought in innovation and team spirit. In the first example, the team successfully explored the available resources and connected them well to create the desired result.

In both cases, we saw the collective wisdom of a team. It proved to be more effective than the wisdom of one person alone. When more than one head work together, the results are multiplied. There is individual excellence in the team, but no one is better than the team as a whole.

16
Walk, Stop, and Start Again

16. Walk, Stop, and Start Again

From rock to rocket

"In the struggle for survival, the fittest win out at the expense of their rivals because they succeed in adapting themselves best to their environment."

– Charles Darwin

Let's come down from the heights of philosophy to the realities of daily life. As I have mentioned in one of the earlier chapters, we were planning a vacation to Goa. We decided to book train tickets to avoid a hectic 14 hour drive. It is a little difficult to get railway reservations during festival times. Tickets may get sold out within a few minutes once the booking opens. We needed 18 tickets in total. So, we decided to divide the task of booking among three of us.

On the day of booking, many surprises were in store for us. Some of us experienced network issues and had to pass the responsibility to someone else. It took a lot of time to enter details of six passengers each. There were a lot of telephone calls, and we ended up with many duplicate bookings and had to be satisfied with two bookings in the waiting list.

We decided to plan better when we book the next time for our return tickets. All seven of us agreed to be on a voice bridge when booking. We decided to create three master lists of passengers in our booking website for each login, which would be readily selected when making the reservation. These two simple decisions made it much easier the next time, when we booked the return tickets.

The journey of humans from rock age to rocket age is full of inspection and adaptation. He learnt from the mistakes and adapted to the environment better. Life is all about consistent learning and improvement. When we look around we can find so many examples of this, the way we travel, the way we communicate, the way we work, and even the way we learn. The very existence of humans is dependent on his ability to inspect and adapt.

With the fielding side

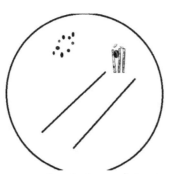

How do we prevent the batting side from scoring big totals? Yes, we must have a plan. We should analyze the other team, their strengths, weaknesses, playing conditions, and hit the ground with a plan. We should select an optimal starting line-up and a balanced team. But, what is the validity of all these preplanned strategies? I will say, only until the first ball is bowled. After that, the team starts creating strategies on the go, based on the situation.

We might have gone into the field with the strategy of attacking the batsmen with close in-fielders. But if our strategy does not work and the batsmen scores well, then we may think of placing more fielders near the fence. If the pitch starts turning unexpectedly, then we replace an established fast bowler with a part-time spinner. If we observe a good partnership developing, then we may consider bringing back our key bowler for a couple of overs. It is all about responding to the challenges and adapting to the situation.

Very often we see on-the-ground team meetings during a match. Many successful teams follow this practice. They conduct quick discussions between the overs to analyze the current situation and to decide on how to proceed. We can find many other examples of this. Something that we always use is the GPS navigation on our car. The moment we miss one route or decide to take another road it recalculates the route based on our current position.

Tailpiece

Both examples above discuss a simple philosophy "Walk, Stop, and Start Again." It is all about inspecting and adapting. Instead of going for a long distance at once and then realizing that we have reached a wrong place, let's cover a small distance at a time. Stop, inspect, and correct our direction.

We always talk a lot about inspection, but often forget that there are changes that result from this inspection. We should be flexible enough to adjust to these changes. The adjustment warrants change in the way we work or even change ourselves. Another aspect here is the frequency of inspection. We should inspect regularly at small intervals so that any deviation from the desired path will come to light at the earliest. At the same time, it should not be too frequent that it affects our work.

Additional Pages

Readers who are not interested in software development can skip this section and go to Chapter 17. Don't worry about this; you can continue the flow from Chapter 17.

Now please read the twelve Agile principles listed in next page. Check if we can map them to the concepts that we have discussed in chapters 5 to 16.

Principles behind the Agile Manifesto

We follow these principles:

Our highest priority is to satisfy the customer
through early and continuous delivery
of valuable software.

Welcome changing requirements, even late in
development. Agile processes harness change for
the customer's competitive advantage.

Deliver working software frequently, from a
couple of weeks to a couple of months, with a
preference to the shorter timescale.

Business people and developers must work
together daily throughout the project.

Build projects around motivated individuals.
Give them the environment and support they need,
and trust them to get the job done.

The most efficient and effective method of
conveying information to and within a development
team is face-to-face conversation.

Working software is the primary measure of progress.

Content in this page is referred from http://agilemanifesto.org

Agile processes promote sustainable development.
The sponsors, developers, and users should be able
to maintain a constant pace indefinitely.

Continuous attention to technical excellence
and good design enhances agility.

Simplicity--the art of maximizing the amount
of work not done--is essential.

The best architectures, requirements, and designs
emerge from self-organizing teams.

At regular intervals, the team reflects on how
to become more effective, then tunes and adjusts
its behavior accordingly.

Content in this page is referred from http://agilemanifesto.org

17
World of Imperfection

17.   World of Imperfection

Pumpkins on a tiny vine

"He put the great heavy pumpkin on a tiny vine and the small mango on a big tree, how foolish the creator is?" The little boy was really confused. Then, a small mango falls on the head that made him think, "What if it was a pumpkin?"

There are different versions of this classic story. But, I don't want to settle for this answer. If we follow this argument, then how can we justify a big jackfruit hanging on the tree? It can cause considerable damage if it were to fall on my head. If we look around, then we can find many examples. Do you think the creator has not done a good job?

The emergency chain

What could be the best way to stop a running train in an emergency? I have not travelled in a train outside India. In Indian trains, it is a chain that is situated on the top of a side wall of each cubicle in the train. Is this the best solution? It is a bit high. Any person who is physically disabled or short in height won't be able to use it. If the train is crowded, then there is a chance of people pulling it unintentionally, when climbing on to the upper berth.

Why can't there be a simple switch that can be easily operated instead? Can't there be a mechanism to talk to the locomotive engineer directly? I can't claim this to be a perfect solution, because considering the technical advances we have made, I doubt if it is the best solution.

The power adapter

When typing in these examples, my laptop battery started flashing the warning symbol. I took my adapter and connected the laptop to the power. All well, but it created another question in my mind. Is this the best design?

The voltage here is 220–230V. The first power cord transmits this to the adapter. The adapter converts this to 19.5V. Another power cord carries this to my laptop battery. Why all this drama? Why can't my laptop battery accept a 220V input? In another way, why can't the laptop have an adapter integrated to it?

The forces

The jackfruit, hanging from the big tree might have confused us. Many forces may influence a decision. There are many other creations to be considered, not only humans. It may not be the perfect solution, but it might be the best solution, considering the forces and constraints.

Same is the case with the emergency chain in the train. It is for emergency purposes and not for normal situations. If we make it easy to use, then there are high chances of misuse. At the same time, there should be "enough" ease of access so that anyone can use it in case of an emergency. Also, when it was developed, the electronics was not as advanced as it is today. I am sure there will be incremental improvements in the future. But, when it was developed it was a good solution, which struck a balance between different forces influencing it.

Considering the power adapter, here the main force is that of generalization. Power standards and socket types differ from one country to the other. So, they have to come with a design that can be customized with minimal effort. For example, to sell it in a place where the socket type is different, only one cord has to be changed. Similarly, it can be customized for different voltage levels by changing only the adapter.

But still, it is not the perfect design. There are many areas of improvements. Why can't we have intelligent adapters for varying input voltage and a convertible plug with an in-built adapter that can be plugged in to any socket types? Here, one of the forces, I assume, will be the cost benefit ratio. What percentage of users travel to different regions? Is there a real demand in the market for this costlier solution?

Go for the best in the given situation

So, it is not the perfect solution; it is the best available solution that matters. Yes, we should pursue perfection, but first let's try the best available solution and fix the problem. After that, we can consider the different forces and decide whether we should spend money in improving on it now or take it up later or never, if the situation doesn't demand it. First, let's go for the best in the given situation.

End Notes

This is an attempt to approach the Agile manifesto and the principles from a different angle. There is no limit to the application of any of these principles. It can be applied from salt to software, from samosa to satellite. It is a way of a life, a better approach. Perfection is something we always pursue, but until we reach there let's make our life better with the available resources. Agile provides a better approach to life.

The moment complexities arise, people tend to stay away, which should not happen.

Let's keep Agile simple.

Work in Progress

> ## Scrum Tales
>
> A collection of scrum stories
>
>
>
> ## Jimmy Kidaram

This is a collection of life scenarios. There are a lot of interesting incidents that we can recollect from our experience with scrum. All these incidents lead us to learning and better understanding of scrum. This book has many handpicked instances.

Backlog

Let's Play Agile

A collection of Agile games

Jimmy Kidaram

Games and team activities play an important role in agile training. I am planning to collect several games that I have personally used in coaching new as well as experienced teams.

www.ingramcontent.com/pod-product-compliance
Lightning Source LLC
Chambersburg PA
CBHW031223050326
40689CB00009B/1452